YOUR KNOWLEDGE HAS VALUE

Bibliographic information published by the German National Library:

The German National Library lists this publication in the National Bibliography; detailed bibliographic data are available on the Internet at http://dnb.dnb.de .

Imprint:

Copyright © 2019 GRIN Verlag
Print and binding: Books on Demand GmbH, Norderstedt Germany
ISBN: 9783668996748

This book at GRIN:

https://www.grin.com/document/492347

Bikal Dhungel

What Are the Factors Influencing Subjective Life Satisfaction? A Case Study of Germany Using the World Value Survey

GRIN Verlag

GRIN - Your knowledge has value

Since its foundation in 1998, GRIN has specialized in publishing academic texts by students, college teachers and other academics as e-book and printed book. The website www.grin.com is an ideal platform for presenting term papers, final papers, scientific essays, dissertations and specialist books.

Visit us on the internet:

http://www.grin.com/

http://www.facebook.com/grincom

http://www.twitter.com/grin_com

SCHOOL OF ECONOMICS

University College Cork - National University of Ireland, Cork

Postgraduate Diploma in Health Economics Practice

Essay Title: Assessment of Factors Influencing Subjective Life Satisfaction

Student: Bikal Dhungel

Introduction

Life satisfaction is considered to be a primary goal of an individual and of a welfare-state. This goal was first proposed by Jeremy Bentham in 1789 with his theory of Utilitarianism which means 'greater happiness for a greater number'. Bentham believed that a state should aim to maximize the level of satisfaction of its citizens because satisfaction is a result of various aspects such as good economic system, social welfare, peace, education etc. This theory has been a very influential one and is still relevant today. Countries place a great value in making its citizens happy and satisfied. Although it has not been employed everywhere, and although social and economic issues exists, places such as Denmark, Finland, Norway have achieved a great success in this matter and rank among the happiest countries. Social, Political, Environmental and other policies of these countries have been envied by others. In Nordic countries plus few European countries, social trust is high, inequality is low, economic development is high, environmental standards are high, people enjoy free education and other index are at finest levels. This, combined, has led to life satisfaction and happiness of the people. With this, it can be concluded that life satisfaction is a multi-dimensional concept and is a result of multiple factors mentioned above. It is also affected by various socio-economic and biological factors. A dramatic change in economic well-being will influence the level. So, it is important to keep these factors in its best form. Hence, interest of researchers to study life satisfaction is obvious and this has led to rich publications around this topic. Based on its nature that it is correlated with diverse factors, studies has been done either relating life satisfaction with individual facts or all factors that might have association with it has been studied. This includes the association with financial success, education, health status, socio-economic status, environment, gender, age, cultural backgrounds and many more. Furthermore, various local, national and international level studies have been carried out frequently. OECD's 'Better Life Index' focuses among others on personal satisfaction level, World Value Survey includes domains related to it and so does the Human Development index. Fulfilling one's goal in life and at the same time, enjoying the privilege of better health, better environment, access to good education, human rights, freedom, good governance and other aspects lead to a happy and satisfied life. Still, national and regional differences exist and these differences has been a major driver of various other studies in the topic. Hence, it would not be wrong to say that 'Life satisfaction' has been a term that still has lots of scope of research although it has been studied intensively in global scale.

This paper will analyse the experiences in Germany from 2010 to 2014 with the data collected through random sampling method for World Value Survey. Due to the limited scope of this paper, I include the below mentioned variables to analyse this in German case. In the first part, I will do literature review of the topic followed by detailed information about data and methodology. After running the linear regression model, I will interpret the results generated and finally move to discussion/conclusion.

Literature Review

Literature in subjective well-being stretches to large number of factors that potentially have association with it. The studies have also been diverse in nature ranging from local to global level and include various socio-economical, biological, environmental, behavioural and technological aspect. Life satisfaction is a two/multiple-way relationship, meaning, a good health might be correlated with happy life and happy life on the other hand can lead to good health (Kavaliauskiene et al 2017). Review of all aspects studied in association with subjective well-being and life satisfaction is beyond the scope of this study. However, the variables included, satisfaction with financial situation, education level etc. has been extensively studied in combination of other factors, gender and age as well. The included variables can yet be further strengthened to analyse deeper information. For example, higher education is associated with more life satisfaction (Del et al, 2011) but it can only be true only if it also yield a better status afterwards (Veenhoven, 1996). Higher education mostly leads to higher income. Cheung and Lucas (2015) found that people with more income than average reported higher life satisfaction but this varies with age. Midlife individuals had higher satisfaction than their young or old counterparts when only financial status was observed. It gives another proposition about the role of age in self-reported satisfaction which tends to reverse the trend. Realo & Dobewall (2011) found older and younger people are more satisfied than middle-aged people in a cross-country comparison in Estonia, Finland, Latvia and Sweden. This might be because middle-aged people face multiple pressures to take care of family including children and parents, have career pressure and other responsibilities according to British Annual Population Survey (ONS) (2018). Another study by Deaton et al (2015) reports that life satisfaction grew with age in English-speaking countries whereas it decreased in low and middle income countries. This study shows a clear pattern of reduction of satisfaction with income with sub-Saharan African countries having lowest level of life satisfaction followed by Latin America and Eastern Europe. Here, the correlation with income, social security system and health can be seen clearly. Within the elderlies, females and males tend to include different domains, with females highlighting relationship with children, social-welfare, partnerships etc. as factors that make them satisfied whereas men tend to focus more on financial situation and partnership (Schafer et al, 2013) Similar findings about gender differences on satisfaction perception were also reported by Oshio (2012) in Japan where the importance of social relations was higher for women whereas financial stability along with other factors for men. This tendency of gender differences stretched to younger and middle-aged women as well. Humpert (2013) found that women in Germany value civic engagement and sport as factors that satisfy them whereas men focused on leisure time activities and hobbies. Joshanloo (2018) found differential tendencies in male and female regarding the domains based on a study done in 150 countries including about one million individuals. The association of life-satisfaction with financial satisfaction and stress has been intensely studied as well. Evidence is unanimous that financial stress reduces satisfaction (Tariq, 2012) (Lantz et al, 2005) and higher financial satisfaction is associated with higher life satisfaction. A 50 year study in Brazil showed that life satisfaction went hand in hand with financial growth and satisfaction (Campara et al,2017) Similar results were mentioned in the findings by Ngamaba & Soni (2017) who studied the phenomenon across different religious groups using World Value Survey with primary focus on religious belief but also on financial status. The World Value Survey data study by Lee et al (2019) comparing US and South Korea found that financial satisfaction significantly affected life satisfaction in both countries. Same phenomenon was also confirmed with taking the sample data from World Values Survey from 1981-2008 for UK where especially the elderly with good financial situation were happier than other groups (Hayes, 2014) Switzerland, Norway, Sweden, Finland and Canada topped the list of most satisfied in financial terms.

There is a gap in literature regarding the association between political stance and life satisfaction. Carroll (2007) found that conservatives are happier than liberals but the definition of conservatives varies widely and once going deeper about why it is so, conservatives tend to simplify things and tend to care less about social inequalities and stick to status-quo (Schlenker, 2011). According to the same report, conservatives are fearful and vulnerable, which can be regarded as negative tendencies, but still, 61% conservatives in the US reported as being very satisfied whereas only 47% liberals thought so (Caroll, 2007). Hence, the available data on life-satisfaction and political stance does not give a clear picture because being satisfied or unsatisfied is limited to its scope, a deeper analysis is required. There is a room further analysis and self-reported studies require other personal traits to be studied as well.

Germany experienced a significant growth of employment level in the last 15 years. Despite the economic crisis of 2008, life satisfaction has risen (Enste, 2014) and despite having a large number of people with some form of mental health issues (Jacobi et al, 2004), the overall satisfaction level shows a good picture with over half of the survey participants choosing the upper tier of satisfaction level. Study by Gray (2014) showed a strong satisfaction level with financial situation in Germany as a whole with western Germany scoring higher than eastern part, which can be attributed to lower level of economic development in the former communist East Germany. National Panel Data survey shows gender differences in satisfaction and this is led by one factor, strong civic engagement, by mostly married German women with children (Meier & Stutzer, 2008) (Humpert, 2013)

Data Methodology and Measurement

The data for this research was taken from World Value Survey statistics about Germany from 2010-2014. World Value Survey is an international network of social scientists whose primary aim is to study the changing values and their potential impact on society and life of people.

Started in 1981, the research designs are of high quality and up to date, it consists of data surveyed in almost 100 countries. (WVS, 2019) Germany was chosen due to its unique economical and societal development recently and due to my particular interest in the country. The World Value Survey was conducted by sending questionnaire to a random sample of population.

The sample size was 2046 which is statistically appropriate for the total population of approximately 82 Million with East and West Germany combined. 24 items were removed as 3 or more values were missing. Participants were directed to fill out the questionnaire sent by post which included a set of about 260 questions categorized in different sections. For this research, six variables were taken as independent variables, namely 'satisfaction with financial situation', 'education level attained', 'health status', 'political stance', 'age group' and 'gender' to see their association with the dependent variable 'life satisfaction'. The dependent variable was subjective life satisfaction which was measured on a likert-scale of 1-10, 1 being 'Very Unhappy' and 10 being 'Very Happy' (Accordingly coded). Same measurement was used for 'Satisfaction with Financial Situation' with 10 being fully satisfied and 1 being fully unsatisfied(Accordingly Coded). Political Stance was also measured in Likert-scale of 1-10, 1 being 'Left' and 10 being 'Right' wing(Accordingly Coded). Age group was in three group likert-scale, 'Up to 29' (Coded as 1), '30-49' (2) and '50 and more' (3). Education level was grouped into nine likert-scale measure, 'No formal education'(1), 'Incomplete primary school'(2), 'Complete primary school'(3), 'incomplete secondary school: technical/ vocational type'(4), 'incomplete secondary school: university preparatory type'(5), 'complete secondary school: technical/vocational type'(6), 'complete secondary school: university preparatory type'(7), 'Some university level education: without degree'(8) and 'University level education, with degree'(9). Gender was measured as 'male' and 'female'. I used as dummy variables, 1 as female, otherwise 0. Health status was measured as 'Poor'(1), 'Fair'(2), 'Good'(3), and 'Very Good'(4). Coding was done from SPSS.

Statistical Analysis

For 'Age' and 'Gender', Frequency Analysis was done whereas for all other independent variables, descriptive analysis was done to explore the given data (See Appendix). Correlation was calculated to see the association between the variables. Bivariate correlation option was chosen. Linear Regression was done with 'Life Satisfaction' as dependent variable and 'Satisfaction with Financial Situation', 'Health Status', 'Education Level Attained', 'Political Stance', 'Age' and 'Gender' as independent variables with 'Gender' put as dummy variable and a confidence internal of 95% was taken. SPSS version 25 was used for all statistical analysis. Total sample size was 2046 of which 15 were excluded for having unanswered more than three or more of studied variables. To analyse the influence on life satisfaction, I estimate the following regression model:

$$\text{Life Satisfaction} = \beta_0\beta + {}_1\text{FinancialSatisfaction} + \beta_2\text{Health} + \beta_3\text{Education} +$$
$$\beta_4\text{PoliticalStance} +$$
$$\beta_5\text{EducationLevelAttained} + \beta_6\text{Age} + \beta_7\text{Gender} +$$
$$\varepsilon$$

Where ε is the Error term.

Results

The frequency analysis was carried to attain survey participant's baseline information. The total number of participants were 2031 among which 50.2% were female whereas 49.9%

were male (1020 females and 1011 males). The majority of subjects were 50 years or more (49.3%). Up to 29 year olds accounted for 17.2% and 30-49 year olds for 33.5% respectively. In terms of educational level attained, the highest number (32.3%) completed secondary school of technical type, 17.8% had a university level education, 22.7% completed primary school and 1.1% had no formal education. The political stance was concentrated around its mean of 4.89 within its standard deviation of 1.79 implying the center-left tendency of the majority. Life satisfaction with a mean of 7.4 shows that majority of people are satisfied with their life. More than two-third of the participants lied in upper tier (7 or more) whereas only about 18% ranked it below 5. The standard deviation was 1.9. Satisfaction with financial situation depicts a similar picture with a mean of 6.55 and standard deviation of 2.3 with over two-thirds being satisfied. Only 30% participants lied within the lower tier of below 5.

Table 1

Descriptives

Descriptive Statistics

	N	Minimum	Maximum	Mean	Std. Deviation	Variance	Skewness	
	Statistic	Statistic	Statistic	Statistic	Statistic	Statistic	Statistic	Std. Error
Life Satisfaction	2029	1.00	10.00	7.3958	1.91295	3.659	-.991	.054
Satisfaction with Financial Situation	2016	1.00	10.00	6.5526	2.33672	5.460	-.540	.055
Political Stance	1863	1.00	10.00	4.8953	1.79787	3.232	.201	.057
State of Health	2030	1.00	4.00	2.8704	.88326	.780	-.389	.054
Attained Education Level	2019	1.00	9.00	5.5473	2.28172	5.206	-.019	.054
Valid N (listwise)	1853							

Table 2

Frequency Table

Gender

		Frequency	Percent	Valid Percent	Cumulative Percent
Valid	Female	1020	50.2	50.2	50.2
	Male	1011	49.8	49.8	100.0
	Total	2031	100.0	100.0	

Age

		Frequency	Percent	Valid Percent	Cumulative Percent
Valid	30-49	680	33.5	33.5	33.5
	50 and more	1001	49.3	49.3	82.8
	Up to 29	350	17.2	17.2	100.0
	Total	2031	100.0	100.0	

Correlations

Correlation coefficients shows that life satisfaction is positively correlated with health status, satisfaction with financial situation and education level attained. When people have better health, satisfaction increases, so does when a person has good financial situation and is higher educated. Political stance does not say much as more than two third of people lied in the middle spectrum of the measured scale.

Table 3

Correlations

Correlations

		Life Satisfaction	State of Health	Satisfaction with Financial Situation	Political Stance	Age	Attained Education Level
Life Satisfaction	Pearson Correlation	1	.384**	.480**	.050*	-.077**	.192**
	Sig. (2-tailed)		.000	.000	.033	.001	.000
	N	2029	2028	2015	1862	2029	2017
State of Health	Pearson Correlation	.384**	1	.210**	.001	-.439**	.259**
	Sig. (2-tailed)	.000		.000	.949	.000	.000
	N	2028	2030	2016	1863	2030	2018
Satisfaction with Financial Situation	Pearson Correlation	.480**	.210**	1	.065**	.072**	.180**
	Sig. (2-tailed)	.000	.000		.005	.001	.000
	N	2015	2016	2016	1858	2016	2008
Political Stance	Pearson Correlation	.050*	.001	.065**	1	.019	-.092**
	Sig. (2-tailed)	.033	.949	.005		.412	.000
	N	1862	1863	1858	1863	1863	1859
Age	Pearson Correlation	-.077**	-.439**	.072**	.019	1	-.165**
	Sig. (2-tailed)	.001	.000	.001	.412		.000
	N	2029	2030	2016	1863	2031	2019
Attained Education Level	Pearson Correlation	.192**	.259**	.180**	-.092**	-.165**	1
	Sig. (2-tailed)	.000	.000	.000	.000	.000	
	N	2017	2018	2008	1859	2019	2019

**. Correlation is significant at the 0.01 level (2-tailed).
*. Correlation is significant at the 0.05 level (2-tailed).

Regression

Table 4

Regression

Variables Entered/Removed[a]

Model	Variables Entered	Variables Removed	Method
1	Gender, Age, Political Stance, Satisfaction with Financial Situation, Attained Education Level, State of Health[b]	.	Enter

a. Dependent Variable: Life Satisfaction

b. All requested variables entered.

Model Summary[b]

Model	R	R Square	Adjusted R Square	Std. Error of the Estimate	Change Statistics					Durbin-Watson
					R Square Change	F Change	df1	df2	Sig. F Change	
1	.550[a]	.302	.300	1.55547	.302	133.305	6	1846	.000	1.895

a. Predictors: (Constant), Gender, Age, Political Stance, Satisfaction with Financial Situation, Attained Education Level, State of Health

b. Dependent Variable: Life Satisfaction

ANOVA[a]

Model		Sum of Squares	df	Mean Square	F	Sig.
1	Regression	1935.171	6	322.529	133.305	.000[b]
	Residual	4466.356	1846	2.419		
	Total	6401.527	1852			

a. Dependent Variable: Life Satisfaction

b. Predictors: (Constant), Gender, Age, Political Stance, Satisfaction with Financial Situation, Attained Education Level, State of Health

Table 5

Coefficients[a]

Model		Unstandardized Coefficients		Standardized Coefficients	t	Sig.	95.0% Confidence Interval for B	
		B	Std. Error	Beta			Lower Bound	Upper Bound
1	(Constant)	2.955	.259		11.405	.000	2.447	3.463
	Satisfaction with Financial Situation	.313	.016	.389	19.002	.000	.281	.345
	Political Stance	.031	.020	.030	1.509	.131	-.009	.070
	Age	.092	.055	.037	1.668	.095	-.016	.200
	State of Health	.649	.048	.305	13.442	.000	.554	.743
	Attained Education Level	.037	.017	.045	2.221	.026	.004	.070
	Gender	.010	.072	.003	.140	.889	-.132	.152

a. Dependent Variable: Life Satisfaction

Residuals Statistics[a]

	Minimum	Maximum	Mean	Std. Deviation	N
Predicted Value	4.3373	9.5025	7.4695	1.02221	1853
Residual	-6.97385	4.77614	.00000	1.55295	1853
Std. Predicted Value	-3.064	1.989	.000	1.000	1853
Std. Residual	-4.483	3.071	.000	.998	1853

a. Dependent Variable: Life Satisfaction

The constant parameter/intercept shows that the mean life satisfaction value would be 2.955 if everything else were 0. Given the P statistics equal to 0.889 for gender parameter, the null hypothesis of being a female will have significant level of correlation with the level of life satisfaction. The correlation analysis shows that life satisfaction level with financial satisfaction and state of health are correlated. So, such regression model might have multicollinearity issue that needs to be checked. In this case, including collinearity statistics and diagnostics did not result in existing issue with multicollinearity (See Appendix, Table 11). High level of significance was shown in state of health, where one unit increase is associated with 0.649 increase in life satisfaction with T-statistics of 13.442 and P-value of 0.000 confirming its robustness. We cannot reject the null-hypothesis that satisfaction with financial situation is in the dependence with life satisfaction with higher than 0.99 degree of confidence. A one unit increase in financial satisfaction will lead to an increase of 0.313 unit of life satisfaction. At the same time, 1 standard deviation increase in state of health and satisfaction with financial situation is

13

associated with 0.305 and 0.389 standard deviation increase respectively. The regression analysis shows that life satisfaction increases by 0.037 units if education level attended increases by 1 unit at 95% significant level. It is also evident that political stance would not have significant effect on life satisfaction. Gender dummy is positive meaning that being a woman increased life satisfaction in this case, however, the coefficient of 0.01 is not significant.

The F-statistics show that changes of the model parameters are significant to explain the changes in the level of life satisfaction. R^2, which measures how close the data is fitted to the regression line is 0.302 in this model. Furthermore, the errors are not auto correlated as the Durbin-Watson coefficient is 1.895, close to 2. So the auto correlation is equal to 0.0525.

Discussion

The regression results shows a strong significant relationship between life satisfaction and subjective health implying that health is an important aspect that contributes to individual's well-being. German government should focus mainly in health sector by providing better care to make its citizens more satisfied. This result goes in parallel with the findings of Kavaliauskiene et al (2017) and Kim et al (2014). The limitation of this study was that people were categorized into three groups with one of which being '50 or over'. Findings by Fitzroy et al (2011) mentions that life satisfaction depreciates with age as people have health issues when they grow older. So, an individualized look into this group with exact age would give better insights about how satisfaction changes when health depreciates when people grow older. Another limitation of the study was political stance, which was not significantly correlated with life satisfaction. Majority of the people lied in the center around the mean. Having a higher number towards the right does not necessarily mean positive and the goal of people, unlike in other variables, was not to increase the number. So, stronger correlation is not relevant whatsoever. Financial situation being one of the primary driver of satisfaction goes hand in hand with other studies including the World Happiness Index, where the list is topped by wealthy nations. However there are outliers as other factors also played a role. With highest per capita income worldwide, Qatar is only at 32nd position whereas much less wealthy Costa Rica is at 13th. Germany's robust economy has contributed to make its citizens wealthy and also finance healthcare system to generate quality care which has significant influence on satisfaction. It has been supported by its free education system in all levels which allows people from all economic background to climb the ladder of higher economic status. This has been consistent with other findings on the topic. This is however conditional on job aspiration of the individual. If the education level attained also enabled the individual to get an appropriate job in the sector, satisfaction can be higher, however, due to the changing nature of job market, if an individual do not get preferred job, it can lead to dissatisfaction. The World Development Report (2019) from the World Bank on the future of job market reports that already now, over 70% people in Europe do different job than what they have studied and within the next two decades, about 50% of jobs will be automatised or are done by algorithms or robots. Hence, right type of education rather than education per se will help to maintain the life satisfaction.

Results of this research are clear evidence that in German case, good healthcare system, future-oriented education and maintaining a robust economy that ensures financial stability of its citizens are important pillars to generate good life satisfaction level.

References

Annual Population Survey, UK (ONS) (2018) Office for National Statistics, https://www.ons.gov.uk/peoplepopulationandcommunity/populationandmigration/internationalmigration/adhocs/008747annualpopulationsurveyestimates Retrieved 3rd Feb. 2019

Bentham Jeremy (1789) taken from 'The History of Utilitarianism', Stanford Encyclopedia of Philosophy. Published March 27, 2009. https://plato.stanford.edu/entries/utilitarianism-history/ Retrieved 2nd Feb 2019

Barry R Schlenker, John R Chambers, Bonnie M. Le (2011) Conservatives are happier than liberals, but why? Political ideology, personality, and life satisfaction. Journal of Research in Personality. https://pdfs.semanticscholar.org/f499/d9f0b60d3abe3c611248775320236311173b8.pdf Retrieved 5th Feb. 2019.

Campara J, Vieira K, Potrich A, (2017) Overall Life Satisfaction and Financial Well-Being: Revealing the perceptions of the Beneficiaries of the Bolsa Familia Program, Brazilian Journal of Public Administration, http://www.scielo.br/pdf/rap/v51n2/en_0034-7612-rap-51-02-00182.pdf Retrieved 5th Feb. 2019

Carroll, J. (2007). Most Americans very satisfied with their personal lives. Gallup report. <http://www.gallup.com/poll/103483/most-americans-very-satisfied- Retrieved 9th Feb 2019

Cheung, F., & Lucas, R.E (2015). When does money matter most? Examining the association between income and life satisfaction over the life course. Psychology and Aging, 30(1), 120-35.

Deaton Angus, Steptoe Andrew, Stone Arthur (2015) Subjective wellbeing, health, and ageing. The Lancet, 2015: 385: 640-48

Del, Mª & Salinas Jiménez, María del Mar & Artés, Joaquín & Salinas-Jimenez, Javier. (2011). Education and satisfaction with life: the role of positional concerns. https://www.researchgate.net/publication/228420014_Education_and_satisfaction_with_life_the_role_of_positional_concerns Retrieved 3rd Feb. 2019

Enste Dominik, Ewers Mara (2014) Life Satisfaction in Germany, Development and Influencing Factors. Institute of German Economic Research. IW Trends Nr-2. https://www.iwkoeln.de/en/studies/iw-trends/beitrag/dominik-enste-mara-ewers-life-satisfaction-in-germany-171266.html Retrieved 8th Feb. 2019

Gray (2014) Financial Concerns and Overall Life Satisfaction: A Joint Modelling Approach. (Use it as comparing study for Germany) https://www.sheffield.ac.uk/polopoly_fs/1.372357!/file/serps_2014008.pdf Retrieved 11th Feb. 2019

Hayes D (2014), What is the relationship between financial satisfaction and happiness among older people ? An analysis using the World Values Survey 1981-2008. Personal FInance and Research Center, University of Bristol, http://www.bristol.ac.uk/media-library/sites/geography/migrated/documents/pfrc1403.pdf Retrieved 5th Feb. 2019

Humpert S, (2013) Gender Differences in Life Satisfaction and Social Participation, MPRA Paper No. 46775, 6. May 2013 https://mpra.ub.uni-muenchen.de/46775/1/MPRA_paper_46775.pdf Retrieved 3rd. Feb 2019

Jacobi F, Wittchen HU, Holting C (2014) Prevalence, comorbidity and correlates of mental disorders in the general population: results from the German Health Interview and Examination Survey (GHS). Psychol Med 2004;34:597–611

Johsanloo Mohsen (2018) Gender differences in the predictors of life satisfaction across 150 nations, Personality and Individual differences, Volume 135 1 December 2018, Pages 312-315 https://www.sciencedirect.com/science/article/pii/S0191886918304392. Retrieved 4th Feb 2019.

Kavaliauskienė, A., Šidlauskas, A., & Zaborskis, A. (2017). Association between Global Life Satisfaction and Self-Rated Oral Health Conditions among Adolescents in Lithuania. International journal of environmental research and public health, 14(11), 1338.

Kim, E. S., Kubzansky, L. D., & Smith, J. (2014). Life satisfaction and use of preventive health care services. Health psychology : official journal of the Division of Health Psychology, American Psychological Association, 34(7), 779-82.

Lantz P, House J, Mero, R, Williams, D (2005), Stress, Life Events, and Socioeconomic Disparities in Health: Results from the Americans Changing Lives Study, Journal of Health and Social Behaviour, Volume 46, Issue 3, 2005.

Lee S, Lee S, Matthew R (2019) Relationship Among Financial Satisfaction, Life Satisfaction, and Political Action: A Comparative Study of the United States and South Korea , Society for Social Work and Research, https://sswr.confex.com/sswr/2019/webprogram/Paper33769.html Retrieved 3rd Feb 2019

Meier, Stephan, Stutzer, Alois (2008), Is Volunteering rewarding in Itself?, Economica, 75(297), 39- 59

Grobe Thomas, Steinmann Susanne, Szecsenyi (2018) 'Schriftenreihe zur Gesundheitsanalyse' (Translation: Report Series on Health Evaluation). Report 2018, Band 7, https://www.barmer.de/blob/144368/08f7b513fdb6f06703c6e9765ee9375f/data/dl-barmer-arztreport-2018.pdf Retrieved 12th Feb 2019

Ngamaba K, Soni D (2017) Are Happiness and Life Satisfaction Different Across Religious Groups ? Exploring Determinants of Happiness and Life Satisfaction, Journal of Religion and Health, Volume 57, Issues 6, pp2118-2139

Oshio, T (2012). Gender Differences in the Associations of Life Satisfaction with Family and Social Relations Among the Japanese Elderly . J Cross Cult Gerontol .27: 259. https://doi.org/10.1007/s10823-012-9169-y. Retrieved 4th Feb. 2019

Realo, Anu & Dobewall, Henrik. (2011). Does life satisfaction change with age? A Comparison of Estonia, Finland, Latvia, and Sweden.. Journal of Research in Personality. 45. 297 - 308.

Schafer Markus, Sarah A. Mustillo Kenneth F. Ferraro (2013) Age and the Tenses of Life Satisfaction The Journals of Gerontology: Series B, Volume 68, Issue 4, 1 July 2013, Pages 571–579

Tariq Qudsia (2012) Impact of Financial Stress on Life Satisfaction, Asian Journal of Social Sciences and Humanities, Vol 1, No. 3 http://www.ajssh.leena-luna.co.jp/AJSSHPDFs/Vol.1(3)/AJSSH2012(1.3-15).pdf Retrieved 3rd Feb 2019

Veenhoven Ruut (1996) The Study of Life Satisfaction. Eotvos University Press 081 2, pp. 11-48 https://personal.eur.nl/veenhoven/Pub1990s/96d-full.pdf Retrieved 3rd Feb 2019

World Bank (2019), World Development Report 2019. The Changing Nature of Work. http://www.worldbank.org/en/publication/wdr2019 Retrieved 9th Feb. 2019

World Database on Happiness Report, (2019) https://worlddatabaseofhappiness.eur.nl . Germany: https://worlddatabaseofhappiness.eur.nl/hap_nat/nat_fp.php?cntry=69&name=Germany&mode=3&subjects=1249&publics=75 Retrieved 11th Feb. 2019

Appendix

Table 6

Frequency Table

Life Satisfaction

		Frequency	Percent	Valid Percent	Cumulative Percent
Valid	2	23	1.1	1.1	1.1
	3	59	2.9	2.9	4.0
	4	63	3.1	3.1	7.1
	5	171	8.4	8.4	15.6
	6	158	7.8	7.8	23.3
	7	345	17.0	17.0	40.3
	8	636	31.3	31.3	71.6
	9	317	15.6	15.6	87.2
	Completely dissatisfied	22	1.1	1.1	88.3
	Completely satisfied	235	11.6	11.6	99.9
	Don´t know	2	.1	.1	100.0
	Total	2031	100.0	100.0	

Table 7

Satisfaction with financial situation of household

		Frequency	Percent	Valid Percent	Cumulative Percent
Valid	2	47	2.3	2.3	2.3
	3	118	5.8	5.8	8.1
	4	132	6.5	6.5	14.6
	5	246	12.1	12.1	26.7
	6	231	11.4	11.4	38.1
	7	371	18.3	18.3	56.4
	8	393	19.4	19.4	75.7
	9	183	9.0	9.0	84.7
	Completely dissatisfied	80	3.9	3.9	88.7
	Completely satisfied	215	10.6	10.6	99.3
	Don´t know	5	.2	.2	99.5
	No answer; BH: Refused	10	.5	.5	100.0
	Total	2031	100.0	100.0	

Table 8

Self positioning in political scale

		Frequency	Percent	Valid Percent	Cumulative Percent
Valid	2	80	3.9	3.9	3.9
	3	267	13.1	13.1	17.1
	4	246	12.1	12.1	29.2
	5	624	30.7	30.7	59.9
	6	269	13.2	13.2	73.2
	7	163	8.0	8.0	81.2
	8	91	4.5	4.5	85.7
	9	19	.9	.9	86.6
	DE,SE:Inapplicable ; RU: Inappropriate response; HT: Dropped out survey	8	.4	.4	87.0
	Don´t know	95	4.7	4.7	91.7
	Left	71	3.5	3.5	95.2
	No answer	65	3.2	3.2	98.4
	Right	33	1.6	1.6	100.0
	Total	2031	100.0	100.0	

Table 9

Highest educational level attained

		Frequency	Percent	Valid Percent	Cumulative Percent
Valid	AU: Inapplicable (No-school education) DE,SE: Inapplicable ; SG: Refused; ZA:Other; Missing	1	.0	.0	.0
	Complete primary school	459	22.6	22.6	22.6
	Complete secondary school: technical/ vocational type	659	32.4	32.4	55.1
	Complete secondary school: university-preparatory type	226	11.1	11.1	66.2
	Don´t know	1	.0	.0	66.3
	Incomplete primary school	142	7.0	7.0	73.3
	Incomplete secondary school: technical/ vocational type	83	4.1	4.1	77.4
	Incomplete secondary school: university-preparatory type	43	2.1	2.1	79.5
	No answer	10	.5	.5	80.0
	No formal education	23	1.1	1.1	81.1
	Some university-level education, without degree	23	1.1	1.1	82.2
	University - level education, with degree	361	17.8	17.8	100.0
	Total	2031	100.0	100.0	

Table 10

State of health

		Frequency	Percent	Valid Percent	Cumulative Percent
Valid	Fair	490	24.1	24.1	24.1
	Good	863	42.5	42.5	66.6
	No answer	1	.0	.0	66.7
	Poor	150	7.4	7.4	74.1
	Very good	527	25.9	25.9	100.0
	Total	2031	100.0	100.0	

Table 11

Coefficients[a]

Model		Unstandardized Coefficients		Standardized Coefficients			95.0% Confidence Interval for B		Collinearity Statistics	
		B	Std. Error	Beta	t	Sig.	Lower Bound	Upper Bound	Tolerance	VIF
1	(Constant)	2.955	.259		11.405	.000	2.447	3.463		
	Satisfaction with Financial Situation	.313	.016	.389	19.002	.000	.281	.345	.903	1.107
	Political Stance	.031	.020	.030	1.509	.131	-.009	.070	.984	1.016
	Age	.092	.055	.037	1.668	.095	-.016	.200	.772	1.295
	State of Health	.649	.048	.305	13.442	.000	.554	.743	.732	1.366
	Attained Education Level	.037	.017	.045	2.221	.026	.004	.070	.907	1.103
	Gender	.010	.072	.003	.140	.889	-.132	.152	.999	1.001

a. Dependent Variable: Life Satisfaction

Collinearity Diagnostics[a]

				Variance Proportions					
Model	Dimension	Eigenvalue	Condition Index	(Constant)	Satisfaction with Financial Situation	Political Stance	Age	State of Health	Attained Education Level	Gender
1	1	6.082	1.000	.00	.00	.00	.00	.00	.00	.01
	2	.466	3.612	.00	.00	.01	.00	.00	.00	.97
	3	.164	6.098	.00	.00	.13	.12	.05	.32	.00
	4	.115	7.286	.00	.02	.45	.22	.07	.06	.00
	5	.092	8.138	.00	.55	.12	.02	.06	.40	.00
	6	.067	9.543	.02	.42	.18	.07	.36	.16	.01
	7	.015	20.184	.98	.00	.11	.56	.46	.06	.01

a. Dependent Variable: Life Satisfaction

YOUR KNOWLEDGE HAS VALUE

- We will publish your bachelor's and
  master's thesis, essays and papers

- Your own eBook and book -
  sold worldwide in all relevant shops

- Earn money with each sale

Upload your text at www.GRIN.com
and publish for free